THE
NERVOUS SYSTEM

Text: Núria Roca and Marta Serrano
Illustrations: Antonio Muñoz Tenllado

El sistema nervioso, nuestro proceso de datos © Copyright
Parramón Ediciones, S. A., 1995. Published by
Parramón Ediciones, S. A., Barcelona, Spain.

The Nervous System copyright © 1996 by Chelsea House
Publishers, a division of Main Line Book Co. All rights
reserved.

1 3 5 7 9 8 6 4 2

Library of Congress Cataloging-in-Publication Data

Bosch Roca, Núria.
  [Sistema nervioso, nuestro proceso de datos. English]
  The nervous system / Núria Roca, Marta Serrano :
illustrations by Antonio Muñoz Tenllado.
    p. cm. — (Invisible world)
  Translation of: Sistema nervioso, nuestro proceso de
datos.
  Includes index.
  ISBN 0-7910-3152-7
  ISBN 0-7910-3157-8 (pbk.)
  1. Nervous system—Juvenile literature. [1. Nervous
system.] I. Serrano, Marta. II. Muñoz Tenllado,
Antonio, ill. III. Title. IV. Series.
QP361.5.B6713   1996   95-12062
612.8—dc20   CIP
                                                   AC

Contents

INVISIBLE WORLD

THE NERVOUS SYSTEM

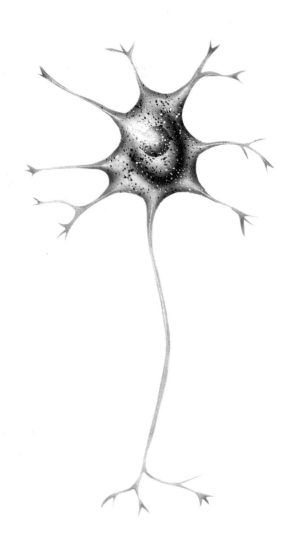

CHELSEA HOUSE PUBLISHERS

New York • Philadelphia

A System for Transmitting Information

Our bodies do not live in isolation from the outside environment. The conditions of the world around us influence our activity and how we function. What happens when the weather is cold? If the body did not detect the fall in temperature and did not act in some way to protect itself, we would lose heat and our body temperature would drop. At low temperatures the body cannot carry out the chemical reactions of metabolism efficiently, and we would die. Instead, we feel the cold around us and our body responds to it: we shiver and get goose pimples. We move to warmer surroundings, put on extra clothing, or sit by a heater. We act to maintain our temperature within limits of comfort and survival.

Information about the condition of our environment as well as conditions within our bodies is detected by means of special cells known as receptor cells, or receptors, which are distributed over our entire bodies. These cells are responsible for translating external stimuli into an electrical impulse. This impulse is transmitted to the body's nerve centers for interpretation by other nerve cells known as neurons.

At the nerve centers, the impulses are transformed into feelings, and appropriate responses are chosen either consciously or unconsciously. These responses are transformed into new nerve impulses, which are then transmitted by means of other neurons to the parts of the body that have been commanded to act, the effector organs.

The central nervous system is responsible for all these functions and consists of nerve centers located in the brain and the spinal cord to receive and interpret stimuli and to originate responses. The peripheral nervous system connects the above-mentioned nerve centers with the receptor cells and the effector organs.

Faced with a change in the environment—for example, a drop in temperature—a sensation of cold is felt. This causes a series of responses. The hair on the skin stands on end (goose pimples), creating a layer of motionless air in contact with the skin to inhibit heat loss. The blood vessels close to the skin contract, restricting blood circulation in an effort to prevent heat from being lost through radiation. We shiver, an involuntary muscle movement that generates heat, and we move around in an effort to raise the temperature of the body.

▼

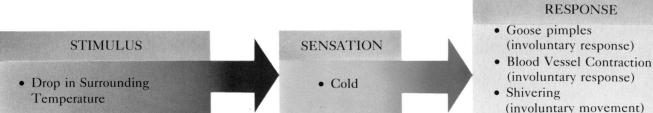

STIMULUS
- Drop in Surrounding Temperature

SENSATION
- Cold

RESPONSE
- Goose pimples (involuntary response)
- Blood Vessel Contraction (involuntary response)
- Shivering (involuntary movement)
- Physical Exercise (voluntary movement)

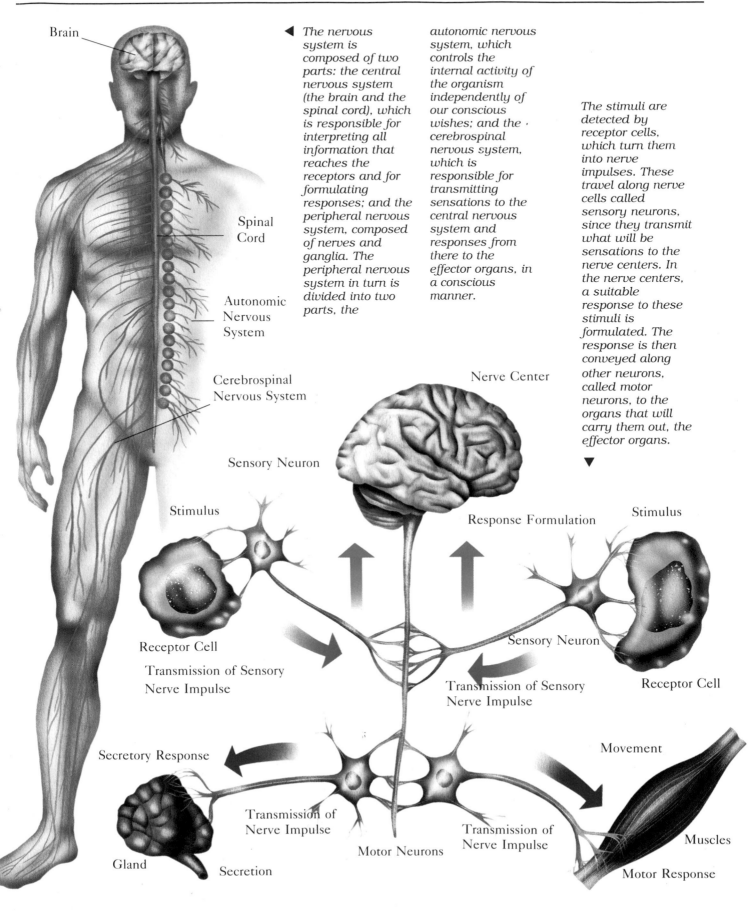

Brain

Spinal Cord

Autonomic Nervous System

Cerebrospinal Nervous System

◄ *The nervous system is composed of two parts: the central nervous system (the brain and the spinal cord), which is responsible for interpreting all information that reaches the receptors and for formulating responses; and the peripheral nervous system, composed of nerves and ganglia. The peripheral nervous system in turn is divided into two parts, the autonomic nervous system, which controls the internal activity of the organism independently of our conscious wishes; and the cerebrospinal nervous system, which is responsible for transmitting sensations to the central nervous system and responses from there to the effector organs, in a conscious manner.*

The stimuli are detected by receptor cells, which turn them into nerve impulses. These travel along nerve cells called sensory neurons, since they transmit what will be sensations to the nerve centers. In the nerve centers, a suitable response to these stimuli is formulated. The response is then conveyed along other neurons, called motor neurons, to the organs that will carry them out, the effector organs.

▼

Nerve Center

Sensory Neuron

Stimulus

Response Formulation

Stimulus

Receptor Cell

Transmission of Sensory Nerve Impulse

Sensory Neuron

Transmission of Sensory Nerve Impulse

Receptor Cell

Secretory Response

Movement

Transmission of Nerve Impulse

Transmission of Nerve Impulse

Motor Neurons

Gland

Secretion

Muscles

Motor Response

Neurons: Links in the Nervous System

The nervous system is basically composed of nerve cells, or neurons, and glial cells, or neuroglia. Neurons are specialized cells that initiate and transmit nerve impulses. The glial cells provide protection and nutrition for the neurons.

A typical neuron consists of the neuronal body, from which there are two types of extensions: the axon and the dendrites, both also known as nerve fibers.

The dendrites are the extensions through which nerve impulses reach the neuronal body. They are usually short, with a wide base, and they end in treelike branches. The axon is the extension along which the nerve impulse is transmitted from the cell body of the neuron to other neurons or other parts of the organism. Normally, it has a narrower base than the dendrites, and its diameter is more regular. Its length can vary from a few inches to a foot.

Some axons have a protective sheath of myelin, formed by a wrapping of glial cells, or Schwann cells, around the nerve fiber. This sheath is not continuous: it has occasional gaps, called Ranvier nodes.

The myelin is very white, in contrast to the gray color of the neurons. For this reason, the parts of the nervous system that are made of neurons are known as gray matter, and those areas where there is a predominance of nerve fibers with myelin sheaths are called white matter.

Neurons are connected to one another and form a complex network of nerve cells similar to the switching mechanisms of a computer. These neural networks can be thought of as computer chips or printed circuits, along which information circulates from one part of the body to another.

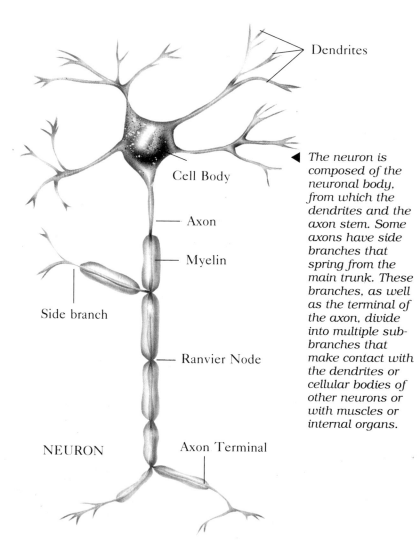

Dendrites

Cell Body

Axon

Myelin

Side branch

Ranvier Node

NEURON

Axon Terminal

◄ *The neuron is composed of the neuronal body, from which the dendrites and the axon stem. Some axons have side branches that spring from the main trunk. These branches, as well as the terminal of the axon, divide into multiple sub-branches that make contact with the dendrites or cellular bodies of other neurons or with muscles or internal organs.*

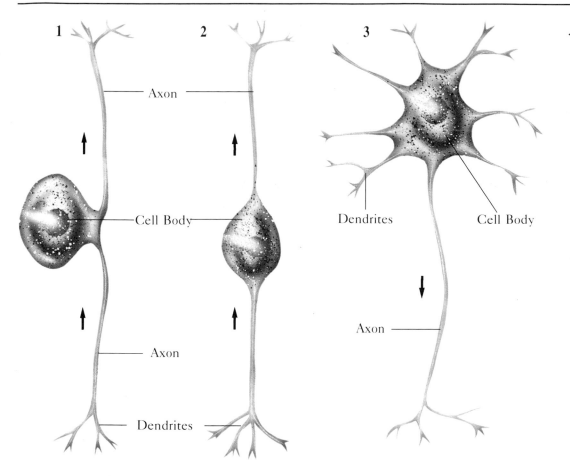

1

Axon

Cell Body

Axon

Dendrites

2

3

Dendrites

Cell Body

Axon

◄ Neurons can be classified according to their length and the shape of their extensions. In unipolar neurons (1), there is only one extension from the neuronal body, which later splits to make a T shape, becoming either a dendrite or an axon. Bipolar neurons (2) have a dendrite and an axon on opposite sides, and multipolar neurons (3) are the most common type of neurons, with various dendrites and a single axon.

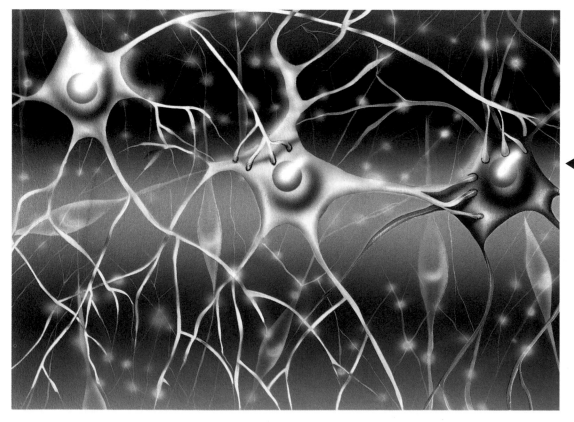

◄ Neurons are interconnected, forming extensive networks along which nerve impulses travel. They are very numerous and form links that join all parts of the nervous system.

The Nerve Impulse

The neuron is the cell that generates and transmits information from one part of an organism to another by means of the nerve impulse. The nerve impulse can be defined as an electrochemical change in the interior and the exterior of the plasma membrane.

Between the interior and the exterior of the nerve cell there is always a difference in the concentration of positive and negative ions. The membrane is thus described as being polarized. When the cell is not transmitting impulses there is a greater concentration of positive ions on the exterior, while in the interior there are more negative ions. This means that between the exterior and the interior of a nerve cell there is an electrical charge called the resting potential.

The nerve impulse is initiated when some factor alters the permeability of the neuronal membrane, causing the positive ions to enter the interior of the cell. If this stimulus is sufficiently strong, the concentration of positive ions inside the neuron will increase until the charge between the inside and the outside of the cell is inverted, a process which is called depolarization. The inverted charge is called the action potential.

The factors that can set off an action potential are very diverse, and may include mechanical injuries such as a prick or a blow, or exposure to cold or heat.

As soon as an action potential is produced in the nerve cell, an electrical current takes place in the areas bordering the membrane. This electric current carries the nerve impulse along the length of the axon. The larger the diameter of the axon, the faster the impulse is propagated. In axons covered by a myelin sheath, the transmission of the nerve impulse is more rapid. This type of transmission is called saltatory conduction.

In axons covered in myelin, propagation of the nerve impulse only takes place in the Ranvier nodes, because the isolating sheath prevents the free entrance and exit of ions along the nerve fiber. This produces the saltatory conduction of the electrical charge from one node to another, which increases the transmission speed of the impulse.

▼

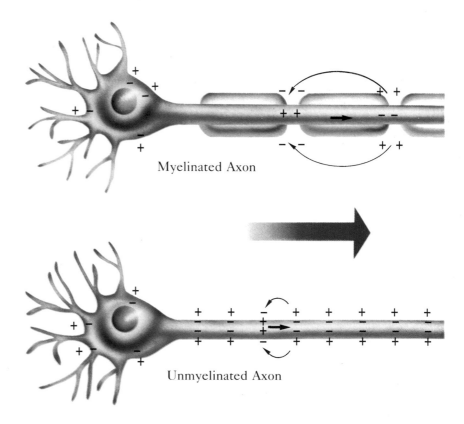

Myelinated Axon

Unmyelinated Axon

The speed of the propagation of the nerve impulse increases with the presence of a myelin sheath (1) around the axon (2). This sheath is formed by extensions of the glial cells (3), and it leaves only the Ranvier nodes (4) uncovered.

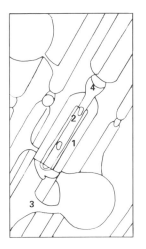

When there is no covering, the action potential is transmitted along the entire length of the membrane, which diminishes the speed of propagation.

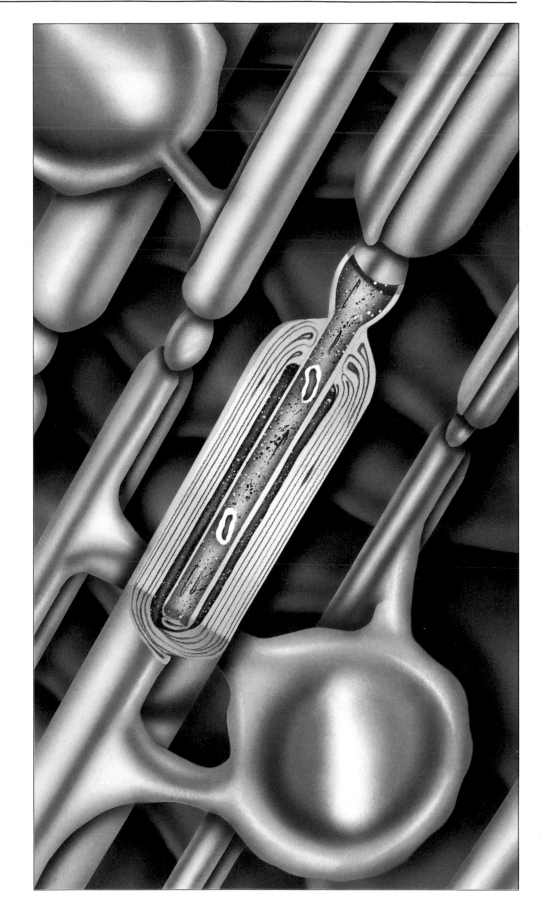

From Neuron to Neuron

The nerve impulse travels through the body along the neurons. However, the neurons are not in direct contact with each other. There is a slight gap between them, which makes transmission of the impulse more complicated. When the impulse reaches the terminal of an axon, it "jumps" to the next neuron across a structure called a synapse. Generally, the contact between two neurons is established between the end of the axon of the transmitting neuron and the ends of the dendrites or the neuronal body of the receiving neuron.

The transmission of the nerve impulse from one neuron to another is carried out by neurotransmitters, chemical substances synthesized by the neurons that are able to alter the permeability of the neuronal membrane. The neurotransmitters are found stored in small vesicles located at the terminal of the axon. The arrival of an action potential causes these vesicles to empty, discharging the neurotransmitters into the space between the neurons. The neurotransmitters cross to the membrane of the adjacent neuron and there they bond with specialized molecules, the receptors. This union causes a change in the receptor membrane, which is stimulated and generates an action potential, thus continuing the propagation of the nerve stimulus.

Neurons receive various types of synaptic impulses. Some are excitatory, which means that they produce an action potential, while others are inhibitory, and have the opposite effect of blocking transmission of the nerve impulse.

The combination of all these inhibitory and excitatory impulses received by a neuron determines whether an action potential will be produced or not.

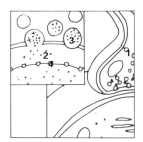

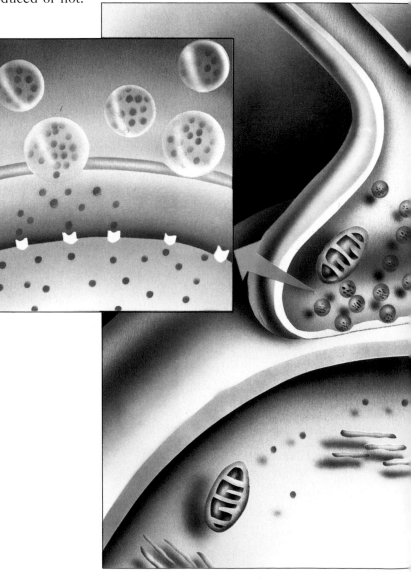

Depending on the type of chemical neurotransmitter that is released into the interneuronal space, the synapse will be inhibitory or excitatory. Under the microscope, the excitatory vesicles usually appear round, while the inhibitory ones are usually lengthened. Synapses can also be classified according to the place where the contact with the next neuron occurs—at the cell body or at the dendrites. ▶

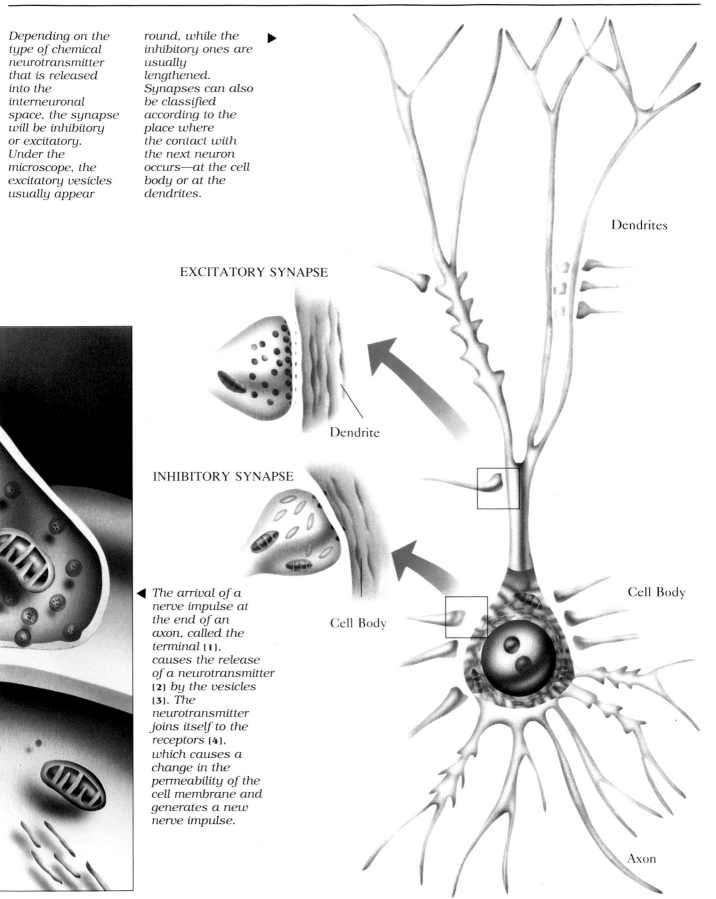

EXCITATORY SYNAPSE

Dendrite

INHIBITORY SYNAPSE

◀ *The arrival of a nerve impulse at the end of an axon, called the terminal (1), causes the release of a neurotransmitter (2) by the vesicles (3). The neurotransmitter joins itself to the receptors (4), which causes a change in the permeability of the cell membrane and generates a new nerve impulse.*

Cell Body

Cell Body

Dendrites

Cell Body

Axon

The Central Nervous System

The central nervous system consists of the brain, the diencephalon, and the spinal cord. The central nervous system regulates the functioning of the different organs of the body, and it is also where the higher mental functions take place. Since it is so vital, the central nervous system is very well protected. Externally, it is covered by bony structures. The brain is inside the cranial cavity of the skull and the spinal cord is protected by the vertebrae of the spinal column, which keeps the body erect.

The central nervous system is also encased in membranes, called meninges, which protect the cerebral and spinal tissue from harmful substances that might be contained in the blood. The meninges act as filters and only allow necessary substances to pass through. Medicines used to treat illnesses of the brain are designed to penetrate these barriers.

The meninges are composed of three layers: the dura mater, the arachnoid membrane, and the pia mater. Among the meninges flows a watery liquid that absorbs sudden movements of the body. It is called cerebrospinal fluid and it also serves a nutritional function because of its high glucose content. The brain has the same density as the cerebrospinal fluid, so that it floats in the fluid. When you receive a blow to the head, the shock is absorbed by the liquid while the brain moves, so that no part of it suffers any distortion.

The cerebrospinal fluid is not continuous around the base of the skull, which is why this part of the nervous system is more susceptible to injury.

The brain and the spinal column are formed of white matter, made up of nerve fibers; and gray matter, made up of neuronal bodies; although in the brain the gray matter is found in the external layer, while in the spinal cord the gray matter is found in the center, surrounded by external white matter.

The meninges are membranes responsible for protecting the central nervous system. They act as a barrier to harmful substances and as a physical support. The dura mater (1) is the top layer and the hardest one. It is found adjacent to the skull (2) and the vertebrae. Between the arachnoid *membrane (3) and the pia mater (4) is the cerebrospinal fluid. The bottom layer is the pia mater, which is in contact with the brain (5) or the spinal cord.*

▼

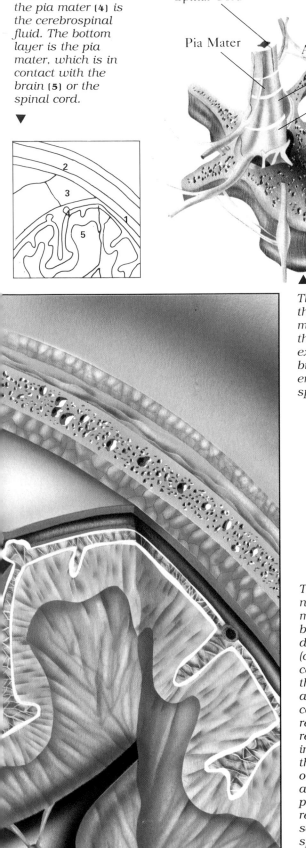

Spinal Cord

Pia Mater

Arachnoid Membrane

Dura Mater

Vertebrae

▲

The dura mater, the arachnoid membrane, and the pia mater extend from the brain along the entire length of the spinal column.

The central nervous system is made up of the brain, the diencephalon (comprising the cerebral stem and the cerebellum), and the spinal cord. The brain is responsible for receiving information from the whole organism, analyzing it, and producing a response, which it sends through the spinal cord.

▶

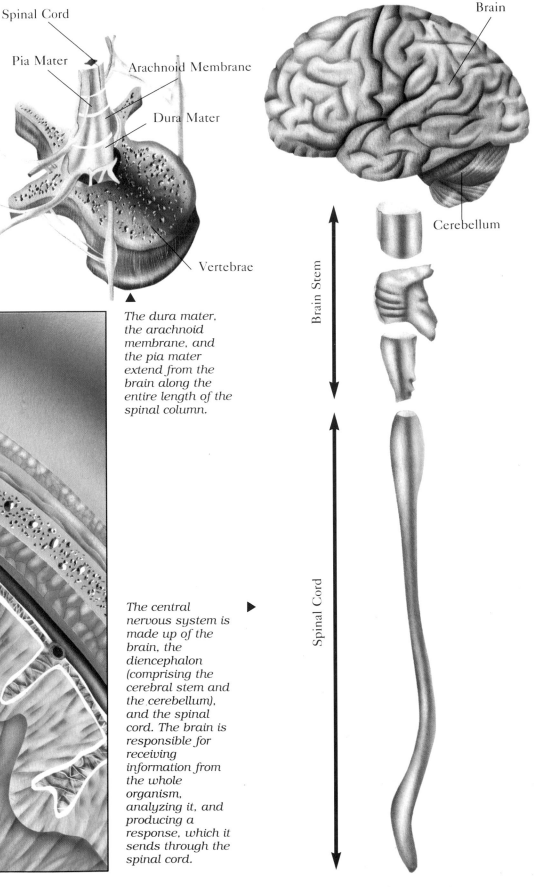

Brain

Cerebellum

Brain Stem

Spinal Cord

The Brain: The Central Processor

As we have seen, the brain is the upper part of the central nervous system and is located in the cranial cavity. Found here are the higher nerve centers that coordinate the senses with bodily movements. The brain is divided into the cerebrum, the cerebellum, and the cerebral stem.

The cerebrum is the largest part of the brain. It is divided into two hemispheres, the right and the left, separated by a cleft called the longitudinal fissure. The two hemispheres are interconnected by a series of nerve fibers that form the corpus callosum. The external surface of the brain presents a series of folds and convolutions, and fissures can be distinguished that separate each lobe, all of which have different functions.

The most external part of the brain is the cerebral cortex, which consists of gray matter. This is where a person's more complex responses are elaborated and where sensations are interpreted. Memory, intelligence, and consciousness are based here. Below the cerebral cortex is the white matter of the brain, where there are localized accumulations of gray matter, called the gray nuclei, the biggest of which is the thalamus. Another important group of these nuclei form the hypothalamus, which is responsible for regulating the hormonal system.

The cerebellum is a gray mass situated just below the cerebrum. It is formed of two lateral portions—the cerebellar hemispheres and an intermediate part called the vermis.

The vermis is involved in voluntary movements and control of balance and muscle tone. In order to perform these functions, it receives information from different parts of the organism and from the nerve fibers of the cerebral cortex.

The cerebral stem is made up of the midbrain, the pons, and the medulla oblongata. It is composed of fibers that connect it with the cerebellum. All these nerve centers have a similar structure, consisting of white matter in the external part, with small islands of gray matter scattered over their surface. The cerebral stem also contains the reticular formation, a mixture of gray and white matter. This structure has opposing effects on motor activity. It can both stimulate or inhibit it.

The brain is formed of two hemispheres, united by the corpus callosum. Below this is found the cerebellum, a nerve center of great importance in the coordination of movement, and the cerebral stem, which consists of three nerve centers—the midbrain, the pons, and the medulla oblongata. ▶

The brain has various fissures known as the sulci and the gyri. Both delineate the cerebral lobes, which are named for the bone that covers them. ▶

Frontal Lobe

Temporal Lobe

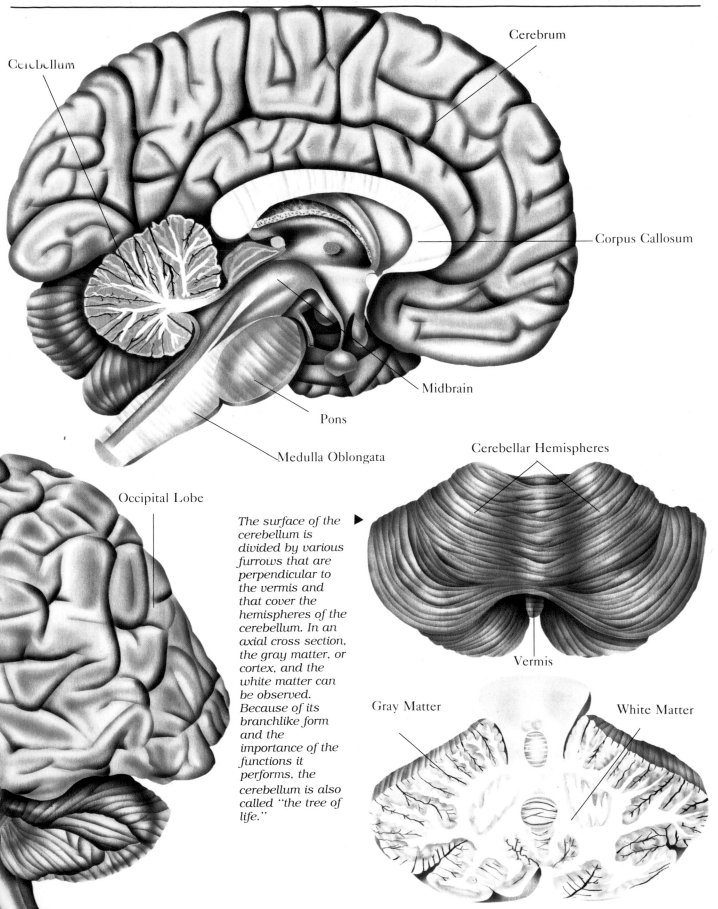

Cerebrum

Cerebellum

Corpus Callosum

Midbrain

Pons

Medulla Oblongata

Occipital Lobe

Cerebellar Hemispheres

Vermis

Gray Matter

White Matter

The surface of the cerebellum is divided by various furrows that are perpendicular to the vermis and that cover the hemispheres of the cerebellum. In an axial cross section, the gray matter, or cortex, and the white matter can be observed. Because of its branchlike form and the importance of the functions it performs, the cerebellum is also called "the tree of life."

The Spinal Cord

The spinal cord provides a means of communication between the central nervous system and the body. It is a long cylinder that stretches from the base of the cerebral stem to the lumbar vertebrae and runs along the inside of the vertebral column in its two upper thirds. In adults it measures approximately a foot and a half in length.

The spinal cord is divided into 31 segments: 8 cervical, 12 dorsal or thoracic, 5 lumbar, 5 sacral, and 1 coxygeal. A pair of nerves extend outward from each segment through the space that exists between one vertebrae and another.

In a transversal cross section, the medulla has an oval shape, with a small depression in the rear part and another deeper one at the front, which forms the ventral or anterior fissure. The external region of the spinal cord is made up of white matter that surrounds a central area of gray matter. The white matter acts like a large conduit for nerve impulses going to or coming from the brain. The central gray matter is arranged in the shape of a butterfly, or an H, and its corners are called horns. This area acts as a center for the distribution of sensory and motor impulses.

In the spinal cord are located neurons responsible for automatic responses, also called reflexes, especially the ones that protect the organism against harmful stimuli such as a prick on the hand. The receptor situated in the skin receives the pain stimulus, which

then travels along the sensory nerve to the spinal cord. Once there, it is transmitted by means of the synapses to the motor neurons, which initiate a muscular response (the contraction of the muscles of the hand, which moves away from the object pricking it) before passing the signal on to the brain. This whole process is called a reflex action.

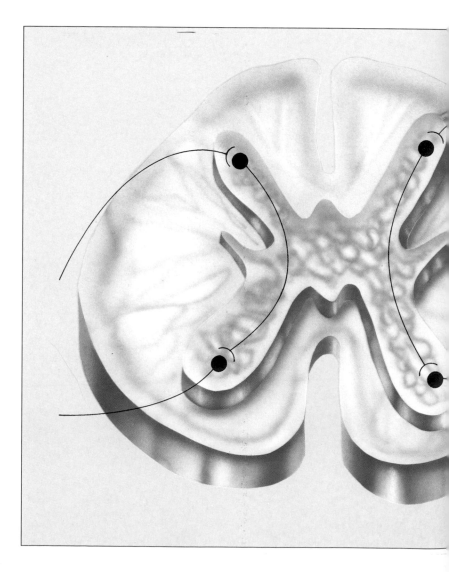

In a transversal cross section of the spinal cord, one can observe the white matter on the outside and the gray matter in the central part, in the shape of an H, with its two ventral or anterior horns and its two dorsal or posterior horns, which are thicker.

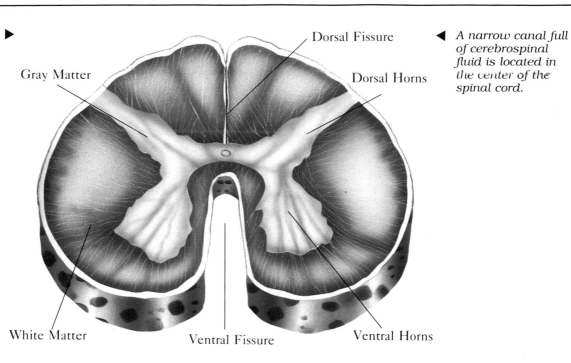

Dorsal Fissure

Gray Matter

Dorsal Horns

White Matter

Ventral Fissure

Ventral Horns

A narrow canal full of cerebrospinal fluid is located in the center of the spinal cord.

Following a painful stimulus (1) the organism responds automatically with a reflex action, in which the response to the stimulus is generated by the spinal cord (2), without passing through the brain. The impulse travels by means of sensory nerves (3) from the receptor to the spinal cord, where it passes to the motor neurons (4), which in turn generate a muscular response (5) that removes the affected area from the point of pain.

Nerves

The peripheral nervous system is made up of nerves that are not found in the brain or the spinal cord. There are two separate networks: the cerebrospinal nervous system and the autonomic, or vegetative, nervous system. The former is responsible for connecting the sensory receptors of the body with the central nervous system and then connecting this with the effector organs so that sensations and responses can be transmitted in a voluntary and conscious way. The autonomic system is responsible for the functioning of the interior organs of the body, and its activity is carried out unconsciously and involuntarily.

Nerves are formed from a great number of nerve fibers, wrapped in connective tissue, which protects them and through which blood vessels run.

Nerves that conduct impulses from the receptors to the central nervous system are called sensory or afferent nerves. Those that carry impulses from the nerve centers to the effector organs are called motor or efferent nerves. Nerves can also consist of both sensory fibers and motor fibers, which are called mixed nerves.

Depending on their point of origin, nerve fibers are divided into cranial nerves and spinal nerves. There are 12 pairs of cranial nerves, which come from the brain and travel to different organs in the head, except for one which goes to the heart and the abdominal cavity. Cranial nerves can be sensory, motor, or mixed. The spinal nerves, which originate in the spinal cord, are much more numerous. There are 31 pairs, and in each pair the two nerves originate in a medullar segment of the spinal cord, one toward the left and the other to the right. These are mixed nerves. As they move away from the spinal cord, they branch into nerves of progressively smaller diameter that penetrate the organs, skin, and muscles.

In the skin, the nerves end in very fine branch endings, with a special structure that holds receptors for touch, pain, pressure, or temperature. There are also sensory nerve endings in the muscles and in the internal organs. In addition, these nerves have motor endings that transmit the impulses that start muscular contractions.

Cranial nerves have sensory, motor, or mixed functions. Pairs I, II, and VIII transmit olfactory, visual, and sound sensations respectively. Pairs III, IV, and VI are responsible for some movements of the eye. Pairs IX, XI, and XII are also motor nerves and are responsible for

Each spinal nerve emerges from the spinal cord in two branches: one comes from the dorsal part (the dorsal root) and the other from the ventral section (the ventral root). They then unite to become the nerve.

▼

Gray Matter

Dorsal Root Fibers

Ventral Root Fibers

Dorsal Root

Ventral Root

White Matter

Spinal Nerves

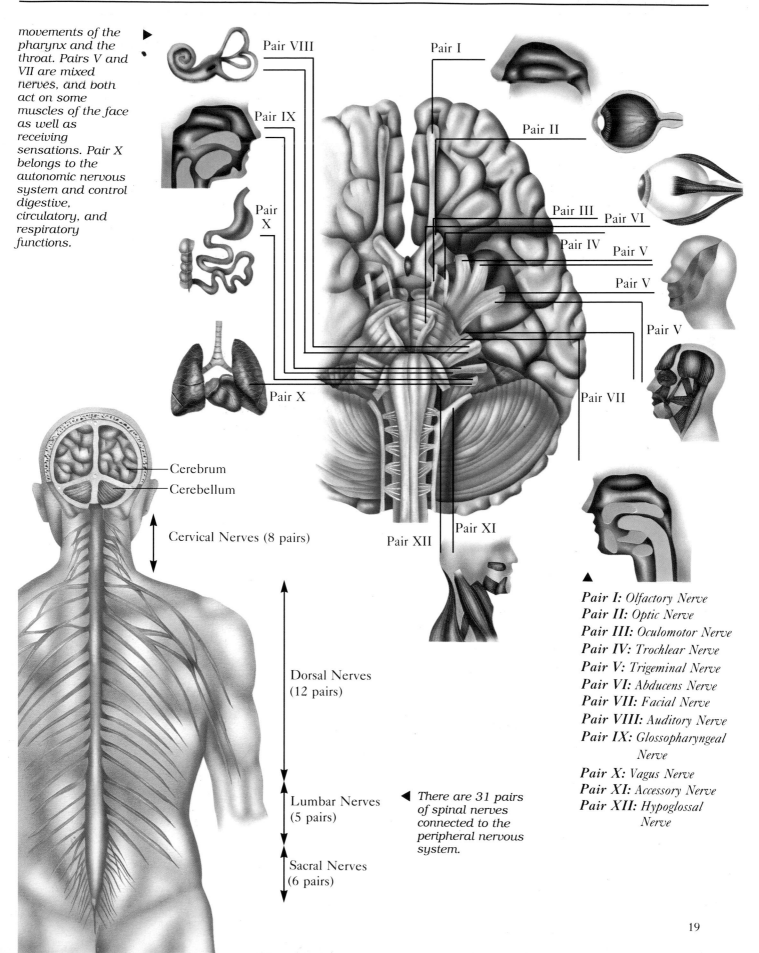

movements of the pharynx and the throat. Pairs V and VII are mixed nerves, and both act on some muscles of the face as well as receiving sensations. Pair X belongs to the autonomic nervous system and control digestive, circulatory, and respiratory functions.

Pair VIII

Pair IX

Pair X

Pair I

Pair II

Pair III   Pair VI

Pair IV   Pair V

Pair V

Pair V

Pair VII

Pair X

Cerebrum

Cerebellum

Cervical Nerves (8 pairs)

Pair XII

Pair XI

Dorsal Nerves
(12 pairs)

Lumbar Nerves
(5 pairs)

◀ *There are 31 pairs of spinal nerves connected to the peripheral nervous system.*

Sacral Nerves
(6 pairs)

▲

Pair I: Olfactory Nerve
Pair II: Optic Nerve
Pair III: Oculomotor Nerve
Pair IV: Trochlear Nerve
Pair V: Trigeminal Nerve
Pair VI: Abducens Nerve
Pair VII: Facial Nerve
Pair VIII: Auditory Nerve
Pair IX: Glossopharyngeal Nerve
Pair X: Vagus Nerve
Pair XI: Accessory Nerve
Pair XII: Hypoglossal Nerve

Receptors

We are constantly receiving enormous quantities of information from the external environment and from our own bodies. The cells responsible for receiving this information are the receptors—sensory cells capable of detecting variations in the internal and external environments and of translating them into nerve impulses. When these impulses reach the nerve centers, they are converted into sensations, which can be conscious (if they involve the cerebral cortex) or unconscious (if they are not routed to the brain or the spinal cord). Typical of unconscious nervous activity is the sensory data from the visceral organs, such as information on the concentration of carbon dioxide in the blood.

Receptors can be either isolated, dispersed throughout the body (like touch receptors), or grouped together to form sensory organs such as the eyes and ears.

There are differences in the various types of receptors. They can be exteroreceptors, which detect changes in the environment such as light or sound, or proprioceptors, which detect changes within the organism, such as muscular tension. There are several different types of receptors that can be distinguished according to the type of stimulus received:

- Mechanoreceptors detect mechanical stimuli and conduct the sensations of touch, pressure, and pain from the skin.
- Thermoreceptors, also located in the skin, detect thermal stimuli, with different ones for heat and cold. These receptors are also capable of detecting pain.
- Chemoreceptors detect chemical changes such as different smells in the nose, as well as sensations of taste. Chemoreceptors in the pituitary detect different gases in the body.
- Photoreceptors are stimulated by light and comprise the cones and rods of the retina.
- Statoreceptors are receptors of balance located in the semicircular canals of the ear.
- Phonoreceptors detect sound and are found in the organ of Corti in the inner ear.

One property that some receptors have is the ability to adapt to stimuli. For example, when you get dressed, the nerve endings in your skin respond to contact with the clothes, but after a while you stop having this sensation. The touch receptors become accustomed to the stimulus so that the sensation loses intensity. The same happens when you get into a swimming pool. At first you notice the sensation of cold, but it disappears after a short time.

Touch, temperature, and pain receptors are spread over the entire body, but they are irregularly distributed. For example, touch receptors are much more numerous in the tips of the fingers than in the back. ▶

In the pituitary or olfactory epithelium are the cells that detect smells—the olfactory receptors—and that transmit nerve impulses to the olfactory lobe. ▶

Light receptors are found in the retina. Among these are the cones, which detect colors when there is sufficient light, and the rods, which adapt themselves better to darkness, although they cannot detect colors. ▶

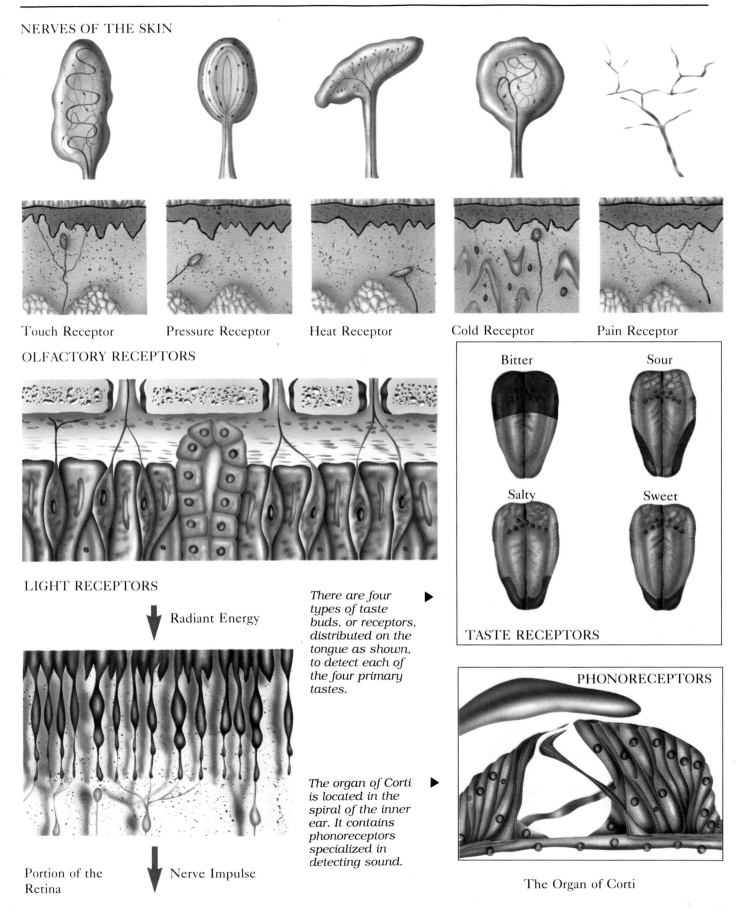

NERVES OF THE SKIN

Touch Receptor

Pressure Receptor

Heat Receptor

Cold Receptor

Pain Receptor

OLFACTORY RECEPTORS

Bitter

Sour

Salty

Sweet

LIGHT RECEPTORS

Radiant Energy

There are four types of taste buds, or receptors, distributed on the tongue as shown, to detect each of the four primary tastes.

TASTE RECEPTORS

PHONORECEPTORS

The organ of Corti is located in the spiral of the inner ear. It contains phonoreceptors specialized in detecting sound.

Portion of the Retina

Nerve Impulse

The Organ of Corti

Control of the Body's Inner Organs

The part of the peripheral nervous system that regulates the internal activity of an organism is called the autonomic or vegetative nervous system. This system controls involuntary actions like the contraction of the cardiac muscle or the secretions of the body's glands. In this way it regulates the internal actions of the body such as respiration, circulation of blood, and the digestive processes.

The autonomic system is composed of nerves that it shares with the cerebrospinal nervous system (some cranial and spinal nerves) and by thick nerve ganglia. The ganglia are groups of neuronal bodies situated on both sides of the vertebral column.

The autonomic nervous system is formed of two parts that have opposite functions. The sympathetic system has its origin in the spinal medulla, and the parasympathetic system originates in the spinal medulla and the cerebral stem.

The task of the sympathetic system is to stimulate the functioning of the organs of the body. It increases metabolic activity and the flow of blood to the brain. It dilates the bronchi of the lungs and the pupils of the eye, activates perspiration, increases blood pressure and cardiac rhythm, and stimulates the rate of secretion of suprarenal glands. The parasympathetic system inhibits or slows down the organism's activity. Both systems interact so that under normal conditions the bodily systems are in equilibrium.

In dangerous situations, the sympathetic system is dominant, so that the organism maintains a state of alertness. At rest, the parasympathetic system is more active.

The autonomic nervous system shares neuronal circuits with the cerebrospinal or voluntary nervous system. The illustration shows how the chains of sympathetic ganglia interconnect with the spinal nerves.

▼

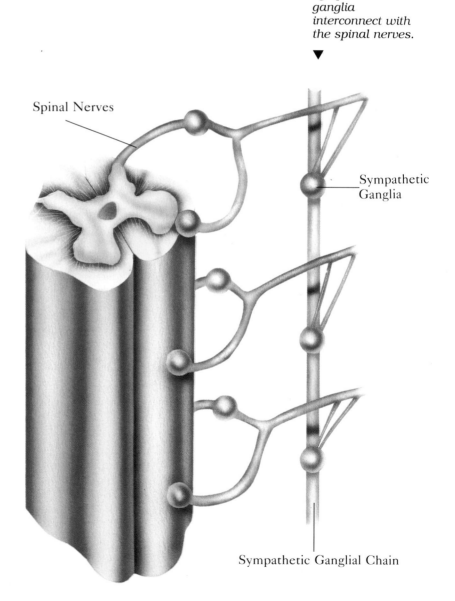

Spinal Nerves

Sympathetic Ganglia

Sympathetic Ganglial Chain

PARASYMPATHETIC SYSTEM

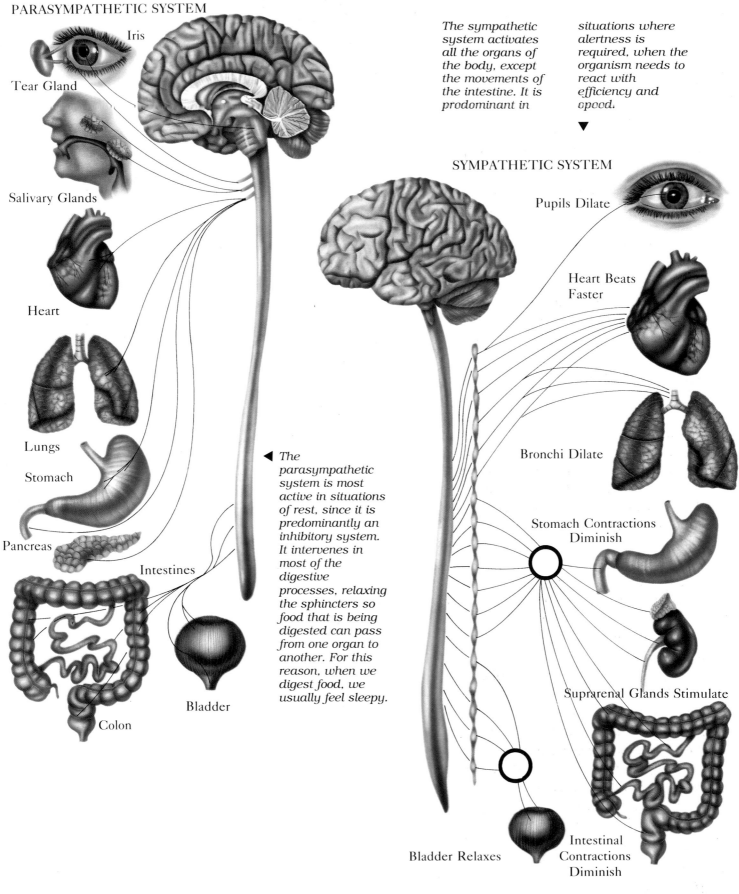

Iris

Tear Gland

Salivary Glands

Heart

Lungs

Stomach

Pancreas

Intestines

Colon

Bladder

The sympathetic system activates all the organs of the body, except the movements of the intestine. It is predominant in situations where alertness is required, when the organism needs to react with efficiency and speed.

▼

SYMPATHETIC SYSTEM

Pupils Dilate

Heart Beats Faster

Bronchi Dilate

Stomach Contractions Diminish

Suprarenal Glands Stimulate

Bladder Relaxes

Intestinal Contractions Diminish

◄ *The parasympathetic system is most active in situations of rest, since it is predominantly an inhibitory system. It intervenes in most of the digestive processes, relaxing the sphincters so food that is being digested can pass from one organ to another. For this reason, when we digest food, we usually feel sleepy.*

The Brain

We have already seen that one of the functions of the brain—more specifically, the cerebral cortex—is to receive and interpret sensations and to elaborate suitable motor responses to them. The sensations that the brain receives from one specific part of the body are not intercepted randomly in the cerebral cortex. There are specialized sensory areas of the cortex associated with each part of the body, as well as specialized motor areas where responses are elaborated.

These sensory and motor areas come under the control of other cerebral functions, such as memory. The sensations that we perceive are memorized, and this allows us to create guidelines for behavior so that we can choose the most suitable response to a certain stimulus. Thanks to our past experience, for example, if we see black storm clouds in the sky, we decide to take an umbrella so that we do not run the risk of getting wet.

The impressions of our experience are recorded in the brain in synaptic networks in the cerebral cortex. It seems that these circuits function differently for immediate memory (in which information is kept for only a few seconds), recent memory (which allows us to remember events that took place a few minutes or hours ago), and remote memory (with which we remember more distant events.)

Memory is linked to many other functions of the brain, including language, for example, which is a kind of code in which words symbolize concrete objects or abstract ideas. In the cerebral cortex there are four centers for language, one for speaking, one for writing, and one for understanding each of these respectively. Language in turn allows us to think and convey ideas. Overall, humans' highest function is probably imagination, the capacity to combine and invent new ideas.

The sensory and motor areas of the cerebral cortex are specifically linked to certain parts of the body, although the area in the brain that they occupy is not proportional to the size of the area of the body that they control. ▶

There are four distinct centers for language in the cortex of the left hemisphere of the brain. Two are for the processes of writing and speaking, and the other two are for the comprehension of these activities. ▼

Spoken Expression

Written Expression

Comprehension of the Written Word

Comprehension of the Spoken Word

Tongue

Vocal Cords

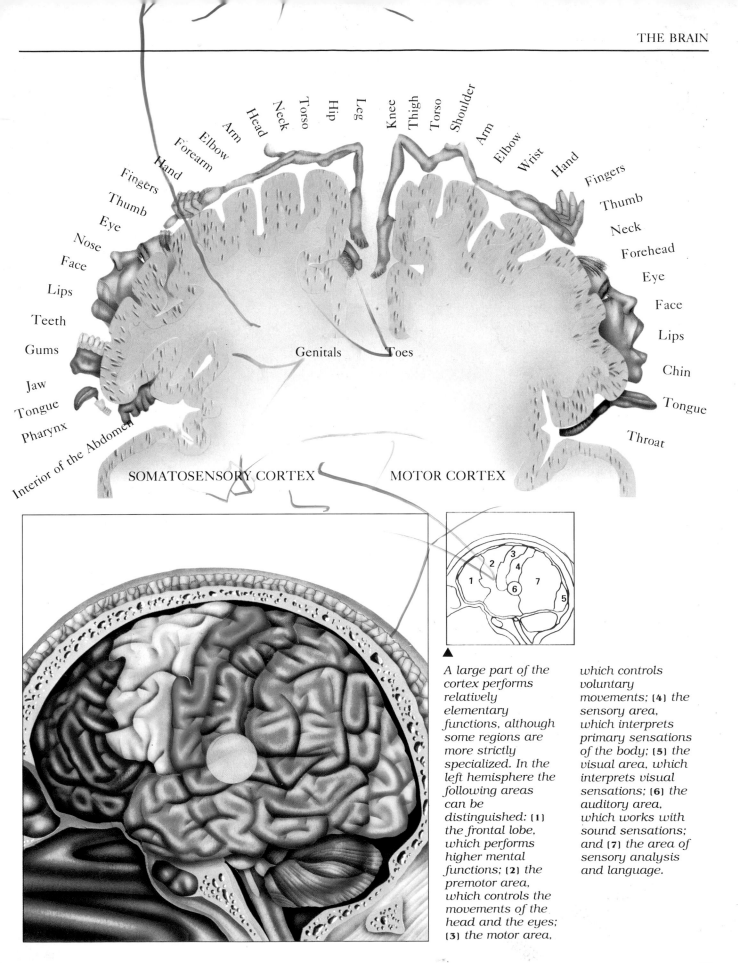

Neck
Torso
Hip
Head
Leg
Arm
Elbow
Forearm
Hand
Fingers
Thumb
Eye
Nose
Face
Lips
Teeth
Gums
Jaw
Tongue
Pharynx
Interior of the Abdomen

Knee
Thigh
Torso
Shoulder
Arm
Elbow
Wrist
Hand
Fingers
Thumb
Neck
Forehead
Eye
Face
Lips
Chin
Tongue
Throat

Genitals   Toes

SOMATOSENSORY CORTEX   MOTOR CORTEX

A large part of the cortex performs relatively elementary functions, although some regions are more strictly specialized. In the left hemisphere the following areas can be distinguished: (1) the frontal lobe, which performs higher mental functions; (2) the premotor area, which controls the movements of the head and the eyes; (3) the motor area, which controls voluntary movements; (4) the sensory area, which interprets primary sensations of the body; (5) the visual area, which interprets visual sensations; (6) the auditory area, which works with sound sensations; and (7) the area of sensory analysis and language.

Emotions and Sleep

Two important characteristics of the nervous system are the ability to generate emotions and the need for sleep.

Emotions are subjective sensations, agreeable or not, involving the entire organism. Fear is an emotion that provokes a negative sensation and a series of physiological effects, including the dilation of the pupils, goose pimples, and muscular contractions. Happiness, on the other hand, provokes an agreeable sensation accompanied in general by muscular relaxation. One's state of mind affects one's external behavior. A state of irritation or frustration can give rise to aggressive conduct.

Emotion is associated with the limbic system, the most primitive structure of the brain, located deep in its interior. This system has connections with other parts of the brain such as the cortex and the hypothalamus, which means that emotions can be moderated or controlled by these structures.

Sleep is a periodic state of loss of consciousness characterized by muscular relaxation and a drop in body temperature and basal metabolism. During its course there is also a decreased rate of cardiac and respiratory activity and a drop in arterial pressure. Sleep is a necessary function. If sleep is repeatedly disturbed, it can cause serious consequences for the individual.

We pass through different phases during sleep. There is light sleep, during which changes in bodily activity are hardly noticeable. In contrast, there is deep sleep, during which these changes manifest themselves in a particularly intense manner.

Furthermore, when we sleep, at intervals of about one and a half hours there are phases of what is called REM or rapid eye movement, also known as paradoxical sleep, during which cerebral activity is as intense, or more so, than in a waking state. These periods are usually between 5 and 20 minutes long, and they usually produce more dreams than any other phase of sleep.

The alternation between sleeping and waking seems to be controlled by the reticular formation, which is a structure of the brain stem composed of neurons arranged in the shape of a net. This formation is also involved in filtering and selecting the stimuli that reach the nervous system, ensuring that monotonous stimuli that do not require special attention do not become a conscious distraction.

Thus, when it is raining, for example, we are not conscious at every moment of the sound of raindrops falling. At the beach we do not always pay attention to the background sound of waves constantly breaking against the shore.

The reticular formation also controls our attention span and our ability to concentrate on specific activities.

The limbic system is the most primitive part of the brain. It is made up of the corpus callosum (1), the anterior nucleus of the thalamus (2), the olfactory lobe (3), the hypothalamus (4), the amygdaloid bodies (5), and the reticular formations (6). Our emotional reactions all

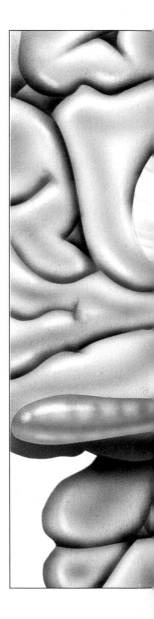

Waking Activity

depend on the limbic system. Because this system is also connected to the cerebral cortex, we have some conscious control over our emotions.

▼

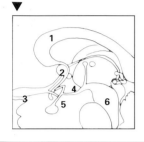

REM or Paradoxical Sleep

◀ *Cerebral activity is measured with an encephalogram, which measures the electrical currents in the brain and draws them on a graph. This makes it possible to determine if there is any alteration in the brain's normal functioning. Encephalograms recorded while awake and during REM are fairly similar, showing that during the REM phase cerebral activity is very high.*

Emotions are accompanied by peripheral responses that create a series of symptoms. For example, fear initiates a series of physiological reactions that make the hair stand on end, the pupils dilate, the muscles contract, and the blood pressure rise.

▼

Narrowing of Thorax — Dilation of Pupils

Dilation of Heart — Bronchial Dilation

Muscular Contraction — Increase in Blood Pressure

Loss of Bladder Control — Suprarenal Secretion

Capillary Constriction

Hair Stands on End

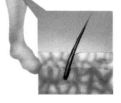

Observing and Understanding

Moving Without Thinking

To observe what a reflex action is, without having to prick or burn your hand, you can carry out the following experiment. Take a small hammer and gently tap your knee in different areas. You will see that when you tap it in a certain place, your leg lifts up without you consciously making it rise. This is because of the existence of a reflex arc between the knee and the spinal cord along which the stimulus travels. Because this circuit has no connection with the brain, your wishes cannot do anything to prevent the movement.

The Body's Alarm System

Pain, the unpleasant sensation we all experience from time to time, might only appear to be inconvenient. However, it is vitally important for the well-being and correct functioning of our bodies. It is an alarm signal that warns us that something in the body is being damaged or is not working properly. Thus, for example, after spending a long time in the sun, we can feel pain all over our skin, which warns us that we are burning our skin and should protect it.

Same Stimulus, Different Responses

Although we have the same nervous structures, we do not all respond in the same way. Individual perception of sensations is subjective. You can easily confirm this by carrying out a survey among a group of friends. Choose several different types of food with salty, sweet, sour, and bitter tastes, with different colors and aromas. Ask your friends about their preferences and dislikes concerning each one. They will probably not give the same answers.

Sweet

Salty

Our Body Gets Used to Almost Anything

As you have discovered for yourself, the body eventually grows accustomed to some of the stimuli it receives. Prove this by filling three containers with water, one hot, one at room temperature, and one cold (with ice cubes). Put one hand into the hot water and the other hand into the cold water. What do you notice after a few minutes? Your hands have become accustomed to the temperatures in both containers. Now put your hands into the water at room temperature. What sensation do you feel in each hand immediately and after a few minutes? The adaptation of the receptors to a stimulus is not immediate.

Hot Water

Cold Water

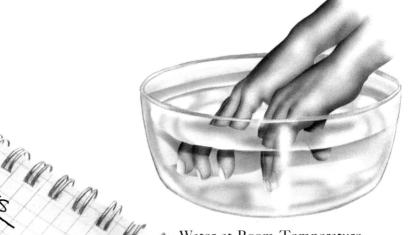

Water at Room Temperature

Bitter

Sour

TASTES

SOUR
SWEET   X
BITTER   XXX
SALTY   X
             XX

SMELLS

PERFUME
HAMBURGER   XXX
ROSE
GLUE   XX

COLORS

RED
WHITE

Glossary

chip *a small integrated electronic circuit*

code *a system of symbols that allows a message to be formulated and understood*

convolutions *each of the folds of the brain, separated by furrows called sulci*

coordination *the organization of various actions so that they work toward a general aim; motor coordination means that the various muscles involved in a movement contract or relax at the right moment and to the correct degree to achieve the maximum precision with the minimum effort*

cranial cavity *the cavity delineated by the skull; the bony box that contains and protects the brain, formed of the upper rear part of the head; the skull consists of eight bones connected to each other by sutures*

endocrine system *the glandular system that produces hormones within the body; the hormones reach the different organs and tissues through the bloodstream and regulate important functions within the body*

gland *an organ that produces one or more hormones or enzymes that act outside the gland*

inner ear *the innermost structure of the ear; it is formed of three cavities that are filled with liquid*

ion *an atom with a positive or negative electric charge*

lumbar *the part of the vertebral column situated between the dorsal and the sacral regions*

metabolism *a collection of physical and chemical processes that are responsible for producing and maintaining the material of the body and generating the energy necessary for survival*

myelin *white fatty material that acts as a protective coating for the conduction of nerve impulses and that covers some axons and dendrites*

nerves *cordlike cells composed of a variable number of nerve fibers (axons and dendrites); they connect the nerve centers with each other*

receptor *a nerve ending whose task is to receive a stimulus and to transform it into a nerve impulse, which can then reach the central nervous system*

retina *the innermost layer of the eye, containing the cells that are sensitive to light*

stimulus *any change in the external or internal environment of an organism that produces a modification in its activity*

synthesize *to manufacture a substance in the body*

Index